HAL•LEONARD® RECORDER SONGBOOK

BROADWAY *Favorites*

2 ANY DREAM WILL DO
Joseph and the Amazing Technicol

3 AS LONG AS HE NEEDS ME
Oliver!

4 CONSIDER YOURSELF
Oliver!

5 GETTING TO KNOW YOU
The King and I

6 I DREAMED A DREAM
Les Misérables

7 MAKE SOMEONE HAPPY
Do Re Mi

8 MEMORY
Cats

10 ON A CLEAR DAY (YOU CAN SEE FOREVER)
On a Clear Day You Can See Forever

11 ON MY OWN
Les Misérables

12 PEOPLE
Funny Girl

13 SUNRISE, SUNSET
Fiddler on the Roof

16 TOMORROW
Annie

14 WE BUILT THIS CITY
Rock of Ages

ISBN 978-0-7935-7228-1

HAL•LEONARD®
CORPORATION

7777 W. BLUEMOUND RD. P.O. BOX 13819 MILWAUKEE, WI 53213

Visit Hal Leonard Online at
www.halleonard.com

ANY DREAM WILL DO

from JOSEPH AND THE AMAZING TECHNICOLOR® DREAMCOAT

Recorder

Music by ANDREW LLOYD WEBBER
Lyrics by TIM RICE

AS LONG AS HE NEEDS ME

from the Broadway Musical OLIVER!

RECORDER

Words and Music by
LIONEL BART

CONSIDER YOURSELF

from the Broadway Musical OLIVER!

RECORDER

Words and Music by
LIONEL BART

GETTING TO KNOW YOU
from THE KING AND I

RECORDER

Lyrics by OSCAR HAMMERSTEIN II
Music by RICHARD RODGERS

I DREAMED A DREAM

from LES MISÉRABLES

RECORDER

Music by CLAUDE-MICHEL SCHÖNBERG
Lyrics by ALAIN BOUBLIL, JEAN-MARC NATEL
and HERBERT KRETZMER

MAKE SOMEONE HAPPY
from DO RE MI

RECORDER

Words by BETTY COMDEN and ADOLPH GREEN
Music by JULE STYNE

MEMORY
from CATS

RECORDER

Music by ANDREW LLOYD WEBBER
Text by TREVOR NUNN after T.S. ELIOT

ON A CLEAR DAY
(You Can See Forever)
from ON A CLEAR DAY YOU CAN SEE FOREVER

RECORDER

Words by ALAN JAY LERNER
Music by BURTON LANE

ON MY OWN

from LES MISÉRABLES

Music by CLAUDE-MICHEL SCHÖNBERG
Lyrics by ALAIN BOUBLIL, JEAN-MARC NATEL,
HERBERT KRETZMER, JOHN CAIRD
and TREVOR NUNN

RECORDER

PEOPLE
from FUNNY GIRL

RECORDER

Words by BOB MERRILL
Music by JULE STYNE

SUNRISE, SUNSET
from the Musical FIDDLER ON THE ROOF

RECORDER

Words by SHELDON HARNICK
Music by JERRY BOCK

WE BUILT THIS CITY

from ROCK OF AGES

RECORDER

Words and Music by BERNIE TAUPIN,
MARTIN PAGE, DENNIS LAMBERT
and PETER WOLF

TOMORROW
from the Musical Production ANNIE

RECORDER

Lyric by MARTIN CHARNIN
Music by CHARLES STROUSE